The Wrightbus, StreetDeck

'driving a greener future'

An in-depth pictorial look at its progressive development from a euro 6 diesel, through to hydrogen and full electric propulsion.

David Barrow

This book is dedicated to the memory of Sir William Thompson Wright CBE, 1927-2022. William along with his father Robert laid the foundations for the company in 1946.

FRONT COVER IMAGE:
Go North East Wrightbus StreetDeck 6356 NK20 ELV is one of thirty-one bought new by the Go-Ahead group in 2020. Twenty-two went to Newcastle-upon-Tyne, with the remaining nine ending up in Oxford. *David Barrow*

TITLE PAGE IMAGE:
An unusual occurrence on the Exceat Bridge, Seaford; two Brighton & Hove Wrightbus StreetDecks on the 12 between Eastbourne and Brighton. A passenger health issue on the leading bus at the Seven Sisters bus stop caused a delay and by the time it was able to continue its journey, the next bus on the service was now following on behind. *David Barrow*

BACK COVER IMAGES:
The two same views, at different periods in history. In this 1935 view we see a Milnes tram belonging to the fleet of Bury Corporation Transport. It is powered by GEC motors, and English Electric controllers. New in 1903, it was reconstructed in 1925, along with others in the fleet, with new top cover and vestibules. *M.J. O'Connor*

The other view, taken in 2021, shows Rotala Diamond Bus North West Wrightbus StreetDeck 40756 MX20 KYJ. *David Barrow*

The Wrightbus, StreetDeck

DAVID BARROW

PEN & SWORD
TRANSPORT

AN IMPRINT OF PEN & SWORD BOOKS LTD.
YORKSHIRE – PHILADELPHIA

First published in Great Britain in 2023 by
Pen and Sword Transport
An imprint of
Pen & Sword Books Ltd.
Yorkshire - Philadelphia

ISBN 978 1 39908 163 4

Typeset by SJmagic DESIGN SERVICES, India.

Printed and bound in India by Replika Press Pvt. Ltd.

Pen & Sword Books Ltd incorporates the imprints of Pen & Sword Books Archaeology, Atlas,
Aviation, Battleground, Discovery, Family History, History, Maritime, Military, Naval, Politics,
Railways, Select, Transport, True Crime, Fiction, Frontline Books, Leo Cooper, Praetorian Press,
Seaforth Publishing, Wharncliffe and White Owl.

For a complete list of Pen & Sword titles please contact

PEN & SWORD BOOKS LIMITED
47 Church Street, Barnsley, South Yorkshire, S70 2AS, England
E-mail: enquiries@pen-and-sword.co.uk
Website: www.pen-and-sword.co.uk

or

PEN AND SWORD BOOKS
1950 Lawrence Rd, Havertown, PA 19083, USA
E-mail: Uspen-and-sword@casematepublishers.com
Website: www.penandswordbooks.com

FOREWORDS

Wrightbus of Ballymena in Northern Ireland have always provided innovative designs for operators in the market, which following deregulation in the UK had been very price sensitive, both in terms of initial purchase price and operating costs. The market has also continued to require quality built in relatively low numbers.

Wrightbus have provided quality bodies on chassis of several manufacturers. But having won the design competition for the New London Routemaster, the company had the opportunity to 'go it alone' as a manufacturer of the total product. This gave them the opportunity to reduce the total vehicle weight, thus reducing operating costs.

For operators on thin margins, the appeal of a manufacturer willing to invest to meet those exacting requirements is obvious. Many operators, including some of the largest, have just not been able to invest in quality new buses needed to maintain a low average age of the fleet. The survival of the UK manufacturing base therefore required to increase sales and the export markets. Many will be surprised to learn of the left-hand drive prototype which has been tested here in the Isle of Man, in France and as far away as South America. This testing led to the Isle of Man (*Bus Vannin*) purchasing ten of the more powerful Mercedes Benz six-cylinder versions, which are now delivering a quality bus service on the Island.

Jo Bamford, who had a vision of the future for the use of alternative fuels, recognised that he needed the whole vehicle design to bring that vision to reality. The sad demise of the long-established family firm of Wrightbus presented that opportunity to speed that vision from dream to reality. This gives the Wrightbus team the future which they deserve to continue innovative designs, which should see further long-term evolution of the StreetDeck double and single deck bus.

Ian J. Longworth
Director of Transport Services, Isle of Man

The Oxford Bus Company has had a long-standing partnership with Wrightbus of Ballymena. Its products have never failed to impress visually, and have consistently met the needs of our business, both double and single deck. Whilst this was traditionally providing bodies on the chassis of several manufacturers (Dennis Dart, Volvo B10BLE and the B5LH), the StreetDeck provided us with the opportunity to buy an integral product.

I took the decision to purchase eleven StreetDecks back in 2015 for our busiest city services in Oxford. Service 5 operated between Oxford Rail Station and Blackbird Leys. We wanted a product with the 'wow' factor on this heavily contested corridor. Nine were painted in a new 'fuchsia' city livery, with two being in the generic Oxford Bus Company red. Feedback was overwhelmingly positive, but the upper-deck front solid corners caused some vision problems for customers.

The Westgate Shopping Centre in Oxford reopened in October 2017 after a major reconstruction, with a new John Lewis as the anchor store. We had extremely high hopes that more people would want to access the city centre using the established Park & Ride system. Westgate had done some research indicating what needed to be improved for this to be true. We therefore wanted to refresh the Park & Ride fleet of buses in their entirety prior to the new Westgate opening, as part of a package of measures to promote bus use. We therefore returned to Wrightbus for twenty more StreetDecks in late 2016, ready for the new shopping centre opening. These were launched at the Divinity School in Oxford, and we incorporated the glazed corners that had caused some difficulty on the City 5 batch.

In 2017, we wanted to upgrade the buses on the City 3 and City 8/9 services, so we ordered another ten StreetDecks with glazed corners. These incorporated an improved interior with some of the customer-centric features that were included on the 'Park and Ride' fleet. This meant that the Oxford Bus Company now operated forty-one StreetDecks.

In 2019 we were successful in winning two new contracts. One for Bicester Village (to provide both station shuttle, and all Park & Ride services) and the other, through sister company Thames Travel, to provide a network of improvements to the Milton Park Science Park in partnership with Oxfordshire County Council. We again wished to order nine new Streetdecks to cover these additional new commitments. But in the end, we had nine new ones diverted from our sister company Go-North East, as they had a batch on order and their needs had changed.

This means we now have fifty StreetDecks in total across Oxford Bus Company and Thames Travel and they deliver an excellent service for our customers day in day out. Some of the Park & Ride fleet have been redeployed onto other services following the COVID pandemic.

In the future as we look to decarbonise our fleet, we hope that Wrightbus, under the new leadership of Jo Bamford, will continue to develop new zero emission products that suit the needs of our businesses, and we look forward to testing these out in the coming years.

Phil Southall
Managing Director, Oxford Bus Company

INTRODUCTION

This book charts the meteoric rise of Wrightbus following the purchase of the company by Jo Bamford, grandson of the founder of the JCB empire, from the ashes of the fall of Wrightbus Ballymena in Northern Ireland into administration on 25 September 2019.

Wrightbus had been developing the concept of a lighter double-deck bus for a few years, an idea first put forward by First Bus. The goal was to reduce the overall kerb weight by up to 1,000kg and be fitted with a euro 6 specification engine, all of which in turn equated to a reduction in fuel consumption.

The bus was built to a semi-integral construction, utilizing four modules, those incorporating the two axles being similar in design to the 1,000 New Routemasters operating in London.

The first five StreetDeck double deck buses built towards the end of 2014 and the beginning of 2015 were built to the revised Gemini 2 design, incorporating the shallow depth upper deck windows. This was all part of the Wrightbus goal to reduce the overall weight of double-deck buses; after the chassis and transmission, glass is the next heaviest component.

Two went to London operators, Arriva and Go-Ahead, and two to First Bus, one to Sheffield and the other Manchester. The fifth one was painted silver and spent a considerable amount of time with Brighton and Hove.

The sixth example built exhibited the greatest change, with a completely new front-end design by Paul Blair, a senior design engineer at Wrightbus. Many sceptics hated it, saying the design was too radical, but by 2016 most London operators had adopted it, but only on the Volvo chassis. It was not until 2018 that the integral StreetDeck started to be specified by a few London operators.

During the past seven years it has evolved from a straight four- and six-cylinder euro 6 Mercedes-Benz diesel engines, to a micro-hybrid, hydrogen and electric and has achieved sales in excess of 1300 units to date.

The three biggest customers of the StreetDeck so far are First Bus, the majority in the Leeds area of West Yorkshire; Diamond Bus North West serving Greater Manchester; and Translink/Ulsterbus in Northern Ireland.

I would like to thank all the photographers, both here in the UK and abroad, who have granted me permission to use their images, and to the many whose names I am unable to acknowledge. I am indebted to the website 'Bus Lists on the Web' and to Wrightbus for allowing me access to their production facility in Ballymena, especially Buta Atwal, Ian Gillott, Kerrie-Anne-Jones, Robert Best, James McNeill, Neil Coulter,

Lee Beckett, Gary Kernohan, and Paul Ainsworth. I would also like to thank Philippa Crofts at Transport for London, Andy Metcalfe 'First Bus fleet asset coordinator' and Darren Hall for all the information and images of Dublin's StreetDecks.

David Barrow
Bury, Greater Manchester
June 2023

Six prototype StreetDecks were built between October 2014 and February 2015. Five had the standard Gemini 3 design, and the sixth had the new radical design that has been the standard on all StreetDecks, except for a few sold outside the UK.

Two of the prototypes went to First Bus, one each to Manchester and Sheffield. The First South Yorkshire example 35101 SN64 CSF is seen in October 2015 at the Meadowhall Interchange on the X78 service. First South Yorkshire would go on to purchase another twenty-two to operate on the same X78 route. This example seen here features a glazed staircase panel, an addition that would prove a popular choice with other operators. *David Barrow*

Arriva London
StreetDeck prototype
SW1 LK64 DVV
at Turnpike Lane
station on service
144 Muswell Hill to
Edmonton Green.

The silver
demonstrator SN64
CTU would spend
a considerable
amount of time with
Brighton & Hove.
It was Brighton &
Hove who took the
first production
examples, a batch
of twenty-four, in
the spring of 2015.
It is photographed
in North Street,
Brighton carrying
temporary fleet
number 703.

The fourth prototype went to Go-Ahead and London Central in January 2015. WSD1 SN64 CTV is seen running out of service from route 12 Dulwich Library-Camberwell-Oxford Circus. This bus was sent to Mexico to demonstrate its potential to 'Ecovia' in Monterrey. On its return to the UK, it had secured an order for five.

The week before Euro Bus Expo 2014, which was to be held at the NEC Birmingham for three days from the 4 November. A press conference was held at the London Transport Museum in Covent Garden. No actual vehicle was present, but photographs showed the radical design of the new StreetDeck. A few days later, 1 November, on the M6 motorway near Wolverhampton the first prototype, destined eventually for Arriva, was spied en-route to Birmingham and the NEC, where it was unveiled to the gathering press the following Tuesday. *Michael Barrow*

On the Wrightbus stand at the Birmingham NEC Tuesday, 4 November 2014; this was the first opportunity for the trade press and operators to examine the finished product. To be fair, the design did not receive 100 per cent approval. In the following weeks and months, a lot of negative comments were written, especially in the letter pages in the transport press, one magazine having some not very complimentary comments in its letter pages, saying it would not sell. Well – 1,500 sales down the line speaks for itself.

Above: Arriva Derby 4600 is seen parked at the Ascot Road depot. This garage was once the home of Derby Corporation Transport, but it was sold to British Bus in 1994, who in turn sold it to the Cowie Group in 1996, who re-branded it as Arriva Derby. In this view it shows to good effect the glazed staircase. *David Barrow*

Opposite above: After its appearance at the NEC, Arriva Derby Wrightbus StreetDeck 4600 FJ64 ETZ finally entered revenue service on 14 January 2015 on route 38 Derby to Sinfin, which is to the south of the city centre. Its specification was 10.469 metres long, with an in-line Mercedes-Benz/Daimler OM934 5.1 litre four-cylinder engine, coupled to a Voith D854.6 automatic gearbox. That combination returned an average of 8.5 mpg. *David Barrow*

Opposite below: Fleet number 4600 is about to enter its stand at Derby bus station on the third day in service. The current bus station was opened in March 2010. It is built on the site of the original Art Deco style bus station that was opened in 1933. The station was eventually closed in 2005 and caused quite a lot of controversy when the decision was taken to demolish the entire structure. Local campaigner Dorothy Skytek spent three months camped on the roof in protest at its planned demolition, all to no avail. *David Barrow*

The first production order for StreetDecks came from Go-Ahead company Brighton & Hove Bus Company, delivery commenced in March 2015. Martin Harris, Managing Director at B&H, explains how that decision came about. 'We looked at what was available at euro 6. We have a complete open mind for the purchase of any new vehicles. I took into consideration the weight saving Wrightbus have built into the StreetDeck and how that will improve on fuel consumption, plus the lead time from order to delivery. Another key factor was the whole life cost of the vehicle, and we wanted something that would roll out the door each morning without any trouble. Wrightbus assured us that the StreetDeck will have one of the best miles-per-litre performance of any vehicle currently on the market.' 923 BX15 OMV was just three weeks old when photographed here at Eastbourne Pier on 11 April 2015. *David Barrow*

The same bus again at Eastbourne Pier showing off to good effect its Ray Stenning Best Impression livery. All twenty-four StreetDecks on the 'Coaster' service are named after people who have some association with Brighton and the surrounding area. This bus is named *Zoe Brigden*. She was known as an 'Aquatic Entertainer' who delighted the crowds on Brighton's West Pier between 1915 and 1924 by diving into the cold English Channel. *David Barrow*

The rear of StreetDeck 943 features an image of the Saltdean Lido opened in 1937 and designed in the Art Deco style by architect Richard Jones. Unlike most Lidos built during that period, this one is still standing. *David Barrow*

Above: **Brighton &** Hove 943 BX15 OMV leaves Eastbourne on 26 May 2015. Just over four years later, the hotel in front of the bus, the Claremont, [just out of view], a catastrophic fire on 22 November 2019. The hotel was completely gutted, and what remained of the structure was subsequently demolished in 2020. *David Barrow*

Opposite above: **Coaster 927** BX15 ONB on the corner of Terminus Road and Grand Parade, adjacent to the Belgian Café, an extremely popular seafood restaurant in Eastbourne. This is a ten-minute service Monday to Saturday, and fifteen minutes on a Sunday, with a journey time of ninety minutes end to end. *David Barrow*

Opposite below: **On Seaford** Road, only four miles from its Eastbourne destination, is *Dora Bryan* 924 BX15 OMW. Dora Bryan was an actor born in Southport, Lancashire in 1923, going on to star in over fifty films and numerous television appearances. Dora and her husband Bill Lawton owned a hotel in Brighton, and it was in Brighton that she died in 2014, aged 91. *David Barrow*

Coaster 943
BX15 ONV *Alfred Richardson* passes the Shore View hotel on Marine Parade, Eastbourne. This is one of the many whitewashed Victorian buildings that grace the seafront in this popular south coast resort. Alfred Richardson was the milkman to the stars who lived in and around the Brighton area. Some of his famous name customers included Laurence Olivier, Dora Bryan, and comedian Max 'There'll never be another' Miller. *David Barrow*

Coaster 929 at the corner of Crowlink Lane and Seaford Road, in the tiny hamlet of Friston, on the outskirts of Eastbourne. *David Barrow*

In this early evening view in May 2015, fleet number 942 *Ralph Reader* crosses the Exceat Bridge over the Cuckmere River on the A259 at Seaford. Plans have been put forward to replace the current steel bridge, During the summer months it is a cause of severe congestion. *David Barrow*

Brighton StreetDeck 927 turns out of the Old Steine inward bound to the Churchill Square terminus. The Old Steine was originally an open green area where fishermen laid out their nets to dry. In the late eighteenth century when Brighton became more fashionable and more buildings began to appear, wrought iron railings surrounded the green. *David Barrow*

923 BX15 OMV at Churchill Square, Brighton about to depart on the twenty-two miles to Eastbourne. The Best Impression green and blue livery is in sharp contrast to the standard red and cream Brighton & Hove colours. *David Barrow*

Coaster 12X *Henry Coxwell* leaves Castle Square/St James's Street on its outward journey to Eastbourne. Henry Coxwell was an aeronaut and writer about ballooning, born in Kent in 1819. He died in Seaford in 1900, which is about 12 miles from Brighton. *David Barrow*

The First Manchester prototype spent some time in South Yorkshire to operate on the X78. 35102 SN64 CSO is seen here parked in Rotherham depot on 7 August 2016. *David Barrow*

SL15 ZGP was another demonstrator carrying the latest bodywork design. It toured the whole of the UK to a wide variety of operators. It was finally purchased by Vision Bus Horwich Greater Manchester in 2019.

In September 2015, Wrightbus launched a low-height version of the StreetDeck, 4.216 metres, as opposed to the full-height version at 4.343. One of the first recipients was the Oxford Bus Company, part of the Go-Ahead Group. Oxford had the need for a low-height double-deck to be able to pass under a low bridge at the railway station. Over the following four years, Oxford amassed a total of forty-seven examples. One of the first in service was 660 SL15 ZGN. *David Barrow*

The First West of England StreetDeck 35109 SO15 CUJ is seen at Bristol Temple Meads station on the 70/71 service, which operates from the railway station to the University of the West of England campus via the city centre.

Bristol 35116
SO15 CVA is here in the city centre on the seven-minute daytime service to the University. These StreetDecks feature micro-hybrid technology, which recovers energy during braking, and stores the energy to power ancillary equipment.

First Leicester 35155 SN65 OKG is leaving the Haymarket bus station on the 14 to Ryder Road and Glenfield Hospital. The new bus station opened in May 2016 and was part of the 'Connecting Leicester Redevelopment Project'. *David Barrow*

First Leicester 35183 SK16 GVD on the 54 Beaumont Centre to Goodwood, seen here on Charles Street, Leicester. 22 July 2016. *David Barrow*

Another Leicester StreetDeck 35186 SK16 GVG micro-hybrid StreetDeck en-route to Goodwood. This bus is only two months old. 22 July 2016. *David Barrow*

The rear of new StreetDeck 35173 SK16 GUF on Humberston Gate, Leicester, 22 July 2016. *David Barrow*

First Mendip Xplorer 35165 SK65 PWL is seen leaving Wells bus station on the 376 Bristol-Wells-Glastonbury-Street service. The name Mendip refers to a local government district in Somerset, and stretches from the Wiltshire border in the east, to the Somerset Levels in the west. Behind the bus is the imposing Wells Cathedral built between 1176 and 1450. In a recent poll it was voted in the top five of the most beautiful and poetic of English cathedrals. *Mark Bearton/Railway Media*

In November 2015, First Bus invested £5m on twenty-two StreetDecks for its fleet in South Yorkshire. 35126 SM65 GFV arrives at the Meadowhall Interchange, Sheffield, having made the journey from Doncaster and Rotherham on 26 November. The livery is based on the old Rotherham Corporation blue, and the silver represents the Sheffield steel industry.
David Barrow

First South Yorkshire StreetDeck 35129 SM65 GFZ route branded for the X78 'Steel Link' service operating between Sheffield, Rotherham, and Doncaster, again at the Meadowhall Interchange, which is connected to the Meadowhall shopping complex opened in 1990, built on the site of a former steelworks, which at its peak in the 1950s employed over 12,000 people.
David Barrow

Midway between Doncaster and Rotherham is the village of Conisborough and its medieval castle. Built in the eleventh century, although partially in ruins it has had substantial investment over the years and attracts around 30,000 visitors per year. *David Barrow*

Some of the roads in Conisborough are quite narrow, with no pavements. 35123 SM65 EFK passes a lone walker with caution close to the nearby castle. *David Barrow*

Go North East X21
'The Castles Express'
StreetDeck 6307
NK16 BXG is about
to leave Bishop
Auckland bus station
on its return journey
to Newcastle,
11 March 2016.
David Barrow

The X21 'Castles
Express' links
Newcastle, Chester-
Le-Street, Durham,
and Bishop Auckland,
all of which have
historic castles,
hence the name.
David Barrow

This side view of StreetDeck 6306 NK16 BXD shows off to good effect the various historic castles between Newcastle and Bishop Auckland. *David Barrow*

Go North East 'Castles' 6304 NK16 BXD is approaching Bishop Auckland bus station, 11 March 2016. All seven buses on this route feature leather seats, tables on upper deck, Wi-Fi and USB connections, power sockets and next stop announcements. *David Barrow*

Above: Although National Express signed a £100m deal with Alexander Dennis in 2014 for the supply of 600 low emission buses over a five-year period to join its fleets in the West Midlands and Dundee, in 2016 they took five Wrightbus StreetDecks. Based in Walsall they were used on the 9 from Birmingham to Halesowen and Stourbridge. No further orders for the type were forthcoming. *David Barrow*

Opposite above: Brighton & Hove took twenty-four low-height StreetDecks in 2016. 810 SK16 GWO is seen here at Castle Square in Brighton city centre on its way to Mile Oak. *David Barrow*

Opposite below: 812 SK16 GWU new in service on route 1 to Mile Oak and Whitehawk via Hove. The Jubilee Clock Tower in the background was built in 1888 in commemoration of Queen Victoria's Golden Jubilee. It is constructed in Portland stone and pink granite. *David Barrow*

Above: **The rear** of 812 showing the different rear end graphics each one carries. *David Barrow*

Opposite above: **B&H StreetDeck** 817 SK16 GWZ turning into St James's Street at Old Steine, 22 July 2016. *David Barrow*

Opposite below: **B&H 821** SK16 GXD carries another full load on St James's Street on the busy service 1 to Whitehawk. Whitehawk is a suburb to the east of Brighton and consists of a large housing estate with over 1,000 dwellings. It was built in the mid-1930s. *David Barrow*

Above: **This Brighton** & Hove 'Coaster Local' livery was introduced in 2021 on route 27, between Saltdean and Westdene. The first StreetDeck in these new colours was 801 SK16 GWC. Seen here in Rottingdean, 16 October 2021, this bus is named in the memory of John Hunt who died in 2017 and served as a Brighton & Hove bus driver for thirty-nine years. *Paul Green*

Opposite above: **'Coaster' 940** BX15 ONS on North Street en-route to Eastbourne. This one is named *Don Partridge* who was a folk singer in the 1960s and lived in Peacehaven. *David Barrow*

Opposite below: **3301 SM65** WNC National Express West Midlands StreetDeck here at Colmore Row in Birmingham city centre. Colmore Row is traditionally the city's more prestigious business address. At around one third of a mile in length, it boasts twenty-three listed buildings. *Phil Tonks*

Above: **Arriva Kent** & Surrey had this low-height StreetDeck, painted in full Arriva aquamarine livery, on long term loan. New in June 2016, 6801 SL16 YPH is seen here in Chatham working the 700 service to the Bluewater Shopping Centre at Greenhithe in Kent. In 2019, it was acquired by Diamond Bus North West in Greater Manchester as fleet number 40714. In 2020 it was transferred to Diamond Bus South East at Stanwell in Surrey. *Darren Walker*

Opposite above: **These next** two photographs highlight the differences in forward vision between the two types of the upper deck front corner pillars. *David Barrow*

Opposite below: **First Bus** has the most StreetDecks in the UK, a number approaching 300, the vast majority in Leeds. The first examples came in 2016 and this one, 35234 SL16 RHJ, is painted in this blue and gold livery for the fast X6 service between Leeds and Bradford. *David Barrow*

Another of the same batch, on the same day, 10 August 2016, in the standard First Bus colours. 35218 SL16 RGX, again on a Bradford to Leeds service, but the 72 route takes fifty minutes end to end, as opposed to the X6 which takes only thirty-five minutes. The Debenhams store in the background was part of the Broadway Centre opened in 2015. In January 2021, Debenhams' new owners announced that all remaining stores would cease trading, and on the 4 May 2021 the Bradford branch finally closed. *David Barrow*

Two Leeds based StreetDecks, 35215 and 35226, climb Nelson Street, Bradford to the entrance to the bus/rail interchange in August 2016. In 2020, Bradford city council announced plans for a £100m project to transform the city centre. *David Barrow*

StreetDeck 35234 SL16 RHJ approaches the interchange on Bridge Street, Bradford on the X6 express service from Leeds. Behind the bus is St George's Hall, a Grade II listed Victorian building opened in 1853. It was partly financed by a consortium of wealthy Bradford wool merchants. In 2016 it underwent a three year £9m refurbishment and is one of only a few major music venues in the North of England. *David Barrow*

Oxford boasts a very extensive 'Park n Ride' system of services. Service 400 to Thornhill is at the pleasant surroundings of the main railway station. *David Barrow*

StreetDeck 669
SK66 HUJ waits at St Aldates between 'Park n Ride' duties, 17 May 2021. *David Barrow*

Oxford Bus
Company Wrightbus low-height StreetDeck 681 SK66 HVF is at the Thornhill 'Park n Ride' site, 17 May 2021. This is also a stop for the Oxford Tube service to London, where commuters can leave their cars and travel hassle free to the capital. *David Barrow*

Oxford 665 SK66 HTY is painted in this red and black livery for the X3 service to the John Radcliffe hospital. In 2020, the new StreetDecks came in these same colours, only this time they were built to the standard height. *David Barrow*

In this view of fleet number 663, it shows the distinctive roof line of the low-height version and those upper deck corner tree branch guards do nothing to improve the appearance. *David Barrow*

In 2016, Reading bought six StreetDecks. The first one was exhibited at Euro Bus Expo 2016 at the Birmingham NEC. It featured a glazed staircase panel and was painted in this striking two shades of orange livery. Fleet number 906 was destined to become SK66 HAS. *David Barrow*

Inside it featured Italian Lazzerini Ethos lightweight seating, glazed roof panels, and a social seating area. They were also equipped with stop/start technology. Each one had a price tag of £216,000. *David Barrow*

Two Go-North East StreetDecks. Orange 6305 NK16 BXE, previously in the blue 'Castles' colours, and 6332 NK67 GOA was in the 'Hop, Tap and Go' promotional livery. *Andrew P. Tyldesley*

Oxford StreetDeck 683 SK17 HHN in the yellow city 3 livery to Kassam Stadium and Science Park. *David Barrow*

Fleet number 690 SK17 HHV on the city service 8 and 9 to Brookes University in Oxford city centre with the Carfax Tower in the background. Sometimes referred to as St Martin's Tower, it is all that remains of the City Church of St Martin, built in the twelfth century. *David Barrow*

Still in Oxford, 691 SK17 HHW is passing Christ Church cathedral, one of the smallest cathedrals in the UK. *David Barrow*

In August 2019, Rotala Passenger Transport acquired the Bolton depot and all its services from First Manchester, in a deal worth £5.3 million. No buses were involved in the deal, but Rotala agreed to lease up to 125 buses from First, until a time when it was able to source new ones, and some second-hand examples from within the Rotala group. The Greater Manchester operation was named Diamond Bus North West and from day one new buses started to arrive in Bolton. Thirteen double-deck Wrightbus StreetDecks, built to First West Yorkshire specification, were snapped up at short notice, along with three ex-demonstrators. The following February, Rotala placed a £30 million order with Wrightbus for 163 new buses, the majority double-deck, and the bulk of the order went to Bolton to serve Greater Manchester. One of the acquired demonstrators '40700 SK17 HHC' was eventually in a special promotional livery for One Smile, a children's charity. *David Barrow*

Towards the end of 2017, Go-North East took delivery of nineteen StreetDecks to operate on the 21 service to Durham, Chester-Le-Street, and Newcastle. The livery and graphics depicted an image of the famous 'Angel of the North' sculpture, designed by Sir Antony Gormley. It was constructed in Hartlepool and weighs 200 tonnes. It is the largest free-standing sculpture in the UK and was completed in 1998. 6320 NK67 GMY is seen crossing the Tyne Bridge, which links Newcastle to Gateshead. The Tyne Bridge was opened in 1928 and is estimated to be held together with 750,000 rivets. *West Yorkshire Bus Spotter*

Above: **Brighton &** Hove next. There were thirty-one StreetDecks of the normal height variety, which entered service between July and December 2017. 841 SK67 FKW is on the 49 to Portslade station. Portslade is a small village on the western fringes of Brighton, and about five miles from the city centre. 841 is named *Thomas Attree* after an important figure in the development of Brighton in the nineteenth century. *David Barrow*

Opposite above: **Brighton &** Hove 853 SK67 FLW en-route to East Moulsecoomb at Churchill Square, 10 August 2019. It is named *Patricia Harding MBE*, a well-known figure in the world of music. She was a member of the Orpheus Choir for over fifty years. *David Barrow*

Opposite below: **London United** Busways is part of the RATP Group (*Regie Autonome des Transports Parisiens*). The company headquarters are in Paris and it was formed in 1949. It now has transport interests in thirteen countries, and employs 64,000 people. London United was acquired by RATP in 2012. WH 45252 SK18 TKY was a demonstrator on a short-term loan in 2018. It is seen here at Euston station '13 October 2018' on the 18 service from Sudbury to Euston via Wembley. *David Smith*

Go Ahead London General StreetDeck WSD 5 SN18 XYX 'out of Merton depot' on Buckingham Palace Road in Victoria, is seen here outside the Grosvenor Hotel, which was designed by architect James Thomas Knowles in 1862, and constructed by Sir John Kelk, who was also responsible for building London's Victoria Station. *David Barrow*

London General WSD 19 SN18 XZO again on Buckingham Palace Road on route 44, Victoria to Tooting station via Wandsworth and Battersea. 3 July 2018. *David Barrow*

Wrightbus StreetDeck HEV demonstrator SK18 TKX is seen leaving Leeds bus station '8 December 2018' on hire to Transdev in Yorkshire. It was used primarily on the 'Aireline' 60 service between Leeds and Keighley. It has subsequently been bought by Rotala for Preston Bus and at the time of writing was still in this demo livery. *David Barrow*

The Tower Transit Group operate franchised bus services in London and Singapore. In London, the company operates out of two depots, with just over 400 buses. In 2019, they took twenty-eight StreetDecks. WH 31104 SN68 AGA is seen here on the M1 motorway on its delivery run from Northern Ireland. *Richard Denny*

Above: **This StreetDeck** HEV 96 mild hybrid (means that it utilizes energy captured during braking to charge the batteries) was once a demonstrator with Arriva London. It was bought by CT Plus in Yorkshire in 2021 and numbered 1904 SK68 TNJ, based at Powell's Rotherham depot. It has lost its London red livery and is now painted white to operate a 'Park n Ride' contract in Doncaster on behalf of the NHS. *Rhys Hand*

Opposite above: **Somerset Passenger** Solutions (SPS) operates community and staff services to serve the construction of the Hinkley Point C nuclear power station. The power station has an estimated cost of £20 billion and is not due for completion until 2025. The SPS fleet consists of 160 buses and coaches, including 35 StreetDecks, all painted white. *Sam Frost*

Opposite below: **In 2019,** Arriva Yorkshire ordered eighteen low-height Wrightbus StreetDecks for the 110 service between Leeds and Wakefield. Only eleven were delivered before Wrightbus went into administration in September 2019. The remaining seven were cancelled and passed to a dealer in West Sussex, still painted in the Arriva Sapphire livery of aquamarine and blue. 1575 SN69 ZXJ is seen leaving Leeds bus station for Wakefield. 26 September 2019. *David Barrow*

At the time of writing First Bus was the largest purchaser of the Wrightbus StreetDeck in the UK, with around 300 examples. By far the greatest concentration of the marque is in West Yorkshire, or to be more precise in Leeds, with close to 200 in service. StreetDeck 35266 SL67 VWS is here seen close to Leeds University. The 'Leeds City' was first introduced in 2018. It carries a two-tone green based livery, with either a red, yellow, blue, green, or grey diagonal front dome colour. This colour denotes which route/district they operate on. *David Barrow*

35306 SN18 XYC is painted in this Elland Road 'Park & Ride' livery. The services utilise the Leeds United FC car park, except on match days when it is used solely by visiting football supporters. *David Barrow*

This is a rear view of the same bus showing off all the benefits of using the service, including its green credentials. *David Barrow*

35302 SN18 XXY is painted in the other 'Park & Ride' livery serving the Temple Green site. Both P&R services terminate at Boar Lane in the city centre. *David Barrow*

StreetDeck 35306
SN18 XYC arrives at Boar Lane on its ten-minute journey from Elland Road.
David Barrow

'Leeds City'
Streetdeck 35546 SK68 TVL stands in a very wet city centre, 16 December 2018, about to depart to Roundhay Park. Roundhay Park is one of the largest city parks in Europe. It covers some 700 acres of woodland, lakes, and gardens.
David Barrow

The Wrightbus, StreetDeck • 57

Another StreetDeck on the same December day, again going to Roundhay Park, but this one – 35530 SK68 TTZ – with blue route branding. *David Barrow*

35506 SK68 TOV is leaving Leeds bus station on the 97 to Guiseley. The town is well known for Harry Ramsden, who in the mid-1930s opened the world's biggest fish and chip shop. It was also the home of the Silver Cross pram factory, from 1936 to 2002. *David Barrow*

A line up of six StreetDecks at the First Leeds Hunslet Park depot, which opened in 2008, and is home to the majority of First West Yorkshire's Wrightbus StreetDecks. *David Barrow*

Again, on the same day, 12 May 2019, three more StreetDecks at Hunslet Park, including one in 'Park & Ride' colours. *David Barrow*

35576 SK19 EZJ on the 50A Seacroft to Horsforth, 19 June 2019. Horsforth is five miles to the northwest of Leeds city centre with a population of 19,000. In the nineteenth century, it boasted the largest population of any British village. *David Barrow*

StreetDeck 35564
SK19 EZU passing
Leeds bus station,
25 September 2019.
The bus station is
the main hub for all
incoming services
across the region
and beyond, which
include all National
Express and Megabus
services. The bus
station in its various
forms has occupied
this site since 1938.
David Barrow

One of the newest
Leeds StreetDecks is
35617 YJ70 BGX. In
front of the bus, just
out of view, is the
Grade II listed Art
Deco Queens hotel,
opened in 1937.
David Barrow

In 2021, First Leeds operated a Sunday and Bank Holiday service from Leeds to Hawes in the Yorkshire Dales, leaving Leeds bus station at 9.15am and returning from Hawes at 3.30pm. *David Barrow*

Two thirds through the journey to Hawes, 35503 SK68 TOA waits at Kettlewell, 23 April 2021. Kettlewell is a village in Upper Wharfedale, North Yorkshire and is a popular destination for hill walkers. *David Barrow*

Above: **35503 SK68** TOA crosses the Kettlewell Beck, a tributary of the River Wharfe. The village is connected to Skipton and Grassington by a network of local buses. *David Barrow*

Opposite above: **Sometime the** unexpected happens. On 28 May 2019, this red StreetDeck was on-tow when a hydraulic equipment failure caused the bus to topple over into a front garden in Hinckley in Leicestershire. Luckily, nobody was injured. A report stated that the bus was returning from the MIRA Technology Park at Nuneaton. This view shows in detail the blue integral subframes. *James Garner*

Opposite below: **In 2019,** Dublin Bus took delivery of nine special double deck buses to test the viability of the current diesel/ electric hybrid buses on the market. The vehicles in question were three each of the Wrightbus Gemini Volvo B5LH, Alexander Dennis Enviro 400H MMC and the StreetDeck HEV 96. The outcome of these trials was that a substantial order was given to Alexander Dennis for its Enviro 400ER plug-in hybrid. Due in some part but not entirely to the situation that had developed at Wrightbus in the autumn of 2019. Dublin Bus StreetDeck WH1 191-D-33234 is seen 10 August 2019 at the Dodsboro terminus on route 25 in Lucan, next to a grotto devoted to the Blessed Virgin Mary. These can be seen all over Ireland, and in France. *Darren Hall*

Above: WH2 191-D-33233, new to Dublin in May 2019, is about to cross the Frank Sherwin bridge over the River Liffey at Kingsbridge. Frank Sherwin was a Dublin politician. The bridge was opened to traffic in 1982. *Darren Hall*

Opposite above: WH1 is on O'Connell Bridge in the centre of Dublin, with an inbound service 25 from Lucan on 13 March 2020, just before Ireland was put in lockdown due to the Covid-19 pandemic. *Darren Hall*

Opposite below: WH1 191-D-33234 on 10 August 2019, crossing the River Liffey in the Dublin village of Chapelizod, close to Phoenix Park. *Darren Hall*

***Opposite*: Preston Bus** became part of the Rotala Group in 2011, after the Competition Commission ruled that Preston Bus' current owner Stagecoach had a near monopoly in the area, adversely affecting competition. They ordered Stagecoach to sell Preston Bus. Eight of Rotala's order for 128 StreetDecks came to Preston, four in 2020, and four in 2021. 40716 BD20 ODF was one of the first to arrive when photographed at the Deepdale Road depot, 1 July 2020. *David Barrow*

***Above*: Preston 40716.** This is the standard interior for all Rotala's new StreetDecks. *David Barrow*

The Oxford Bus Company's nine new StreetDecks started to arrive in July 2020. These nine were built to full-height; all the others in Oxford are of low-height configuration. The nine were part of an order for thirty-one for Go North East, but due to a change of plan at Gateshead, nine examples went south. 902 NK20 EKW awaits its next journey in St Aldates, Oxford. *David Barrow*

Oxford Bus Company fleet number 902 is leaving the city on the X13 to the John Radcliffe hospital. Each of these nine are built to a high specification, with glazed staircase, USB ports, wireless charging points and tables. *David Barrow*

O.B.C. 901 NK20 EKT is passing St Nicolas Parish Church in Abingdon on the X3 service, 22 April 2021. *Jack Cooper*

Thames Travel was a private company founded in 1998 with four buses. In 2011 it was bought by the Go-Ahead Group and the fleet now consists of eighty buses and is numbered with Oxford Bus fleet numbers. Six of the nine new StreetDecks have been allocated to Thames Travel. 905 NK20 EKP. *David Barrow*

Above: **The 'Connector'** two-tone grey brand is used for Didcot focused services. The X2 starts at Oxford railway station via Abingdon to Didcot. 906 NK20 EKR waits at St Aldates. *David Barrow*

Opposite: **Thames Travel** StreetDeck 905 NK20 EKP passing Christ Church Cathedral in St Aldates, Oxford. *David Barrow*

Above: Bus Vannin is the government owned bus service provider on the Isle of Man. In 2020, they took delivery of ten of the more powerful 7.7 litre, six-cylinder Daimler OM936 engine. The reason for this is that Bus Vannin operate a high speed, hilly network of services, so they needed the extra power the standard OM934 engine could not deliver. The bigger engine has a higher top speed of 62 mph, and also comes with third generation micro-hybrid technology. The two engines OM934 and OM936. The O stands for oil, and the M for Mercedes-Benz. The 9 is the engine series number, and the 4 or 6 is the number of cylinders. Fleet number 303 PMN 303E is seen here at the Wrightbus Ballymena factory before delivery. *Wrightbus*

Opposite above: 309 PMN 309E is parked above Douglas Harbour, with an Isle of Man Steam Packet Company ferry seen loading for its journey to Heysham. *Richard Cranmer*

Opposite below: In this nearside rear view, 309 shows the extra length of the rear engine compartment needed to accommodate the bigger six-cylinder engine, and a much larger top deck rear window. *Richard Cranmer*

***Opposite above*: In 2019,** Go North East ordered thirty-one Wrightbus StreetDecks; nine were diverted to the Oxford Bus Company, a fellow Go-Ahead Company. The remaining twenty-two were finished in variations of the 'X-lines' branding, a fast direct service with free Wi-Fi and next stop announcements. 6365 NK70 BYB is on the X1 service. *David Barrow*

***Opposite below*: This rear** three quarter view of 6365 shows to good effect how the vivid red colour blends in well with the gold. *David Barrow*

***Above*: 'X-lines' X1** 6375 NK70 BYT has just left Eldon Square bus station to Gateshead, Washington and Easington Lane. *David Barrow*

Above: 6359 NK20 EMJ about to enter Eldon Square bus station on the X45 from Consett, Shotley Bridge and the Gateshead Metrocentre. 14 September 2020. *David Barrow*

Opposite: The same bus, the same route, but a different time of day and location. 6359 NK20 EMJ is on the corner of Newgate Street and Grainger Street, outward bound on its sixteen-mile journey to Consett. *David Barrow*

Above: **First Aberdeen** made history on 28 January 2021, being the first operator anywhere to put hydrogen double deck buses into service with a total of fifteen in a joint project with First Bus, Aberdeen City Council, the Scottish Government, and the European Union, representing a total investment of £8.3 million. 39702 SV70 BWL is photographed outside the 1906 built His Majesty's Theatre in the city centre. *First Aberdeen/Michal Wachucik/Abermedia*

Opposite: **Same bus** at a different location. This time the building is Marischal College. Since 2011, it has acted as the headquarters of Aberdeen City Council; before that it was part of the University of Aberdeen, which still uses part of the building. In the thirteen-week period since their introduction to the end of April 2021, the combined fleet of fifteen have operated a total of 100,000 miles, which equates to just over 6,500 miles per bus. This has saved 170,000kg of CO2 from being released into the atmosphere. *First Aberdeen/Michal Wachucik/abermedia*

The first London operator to receive hydrogen powered StreetDecks was Metroline (a subsidiary of the ComfortDelGro Corporation based in Singapore) which is operating twenty out of its Perivale depot in West London. All twenty are owned by Transport for London and leased to Metroline. The total cost for the buses, plus fuelling infrastructure, came to £12 million. £5 million came from the European Commission and £1 million from the Office for Low Emission Vehicles [OLEV]. That equates to each bus costing in the region of £500,000 each. WHD 2725 LK70 AZV is on route 7 to East Acton. *London Transport 65*

Metroline hydrogen powered StreetDeck FCEV {Fuel-Cell Electric Vehicle} WHD 2726 LK70 AZW on Brunel Road in East Acton, 24 May 2021. In the space usually occupied by the engine is the Ballard fuel cell. Above that are six hydrogen cylinders. The top two cylinders are behind the rear seats on the upper deck. Of particular interest is that these are the first Metroline double decks to be fitted with cameras instead of rear-view mirrors. *Richard Thomas*

Ensign Bus of Purfleet Essex took seven of these low-height StreetDecks in March 2021. They were a cancelled order from Arriva Yorkshire. 166 LX21 CHO is parked outside the company's headquarters. *David Storey/Ensign Bus*

Preston Bus
StreetDeck 40806
BX21 DFD was new in
May 2021 and is seen
at journey's end at
the ASDA superstore
at Fulwood.
David Barrow

Preston Bus 40808
BX21 DFF on the 23
service connecting
the bus station to
the Royal Preston
Hospital, the
University of Central
Lancashire, and the
ASDA superstore
at Fulwood.
David Barrow

Three hydrogen powered Wrightbus StreetDeck FCEVs were supplied to Transport for Ireland for trials in Dublin. At first they went to Bus Eireann, before moving to Dublin Bus. One of the three – HWD2 211-D-24853 – made a brief visit to Broadstone depot to be inspected by engineering staff. The bus has also been viewed by the Dublin Fire and Rescue Service. They wanted to establish what to do if the worst-case scenario should happen. The Broadstone site was once the Dublin terminus for the Midland and Great Western Railway. In fact, the main station building, which was built in 1850, is now the headquarters of Bus Eireann. *Darren Hall*

The first new buses that Diamond Bus North West acquired were the thirteen First Bus spec Wrightbus StreetDecks. 40707 SO19 MVX had only five days in service when photographed in Bury town centre on the 471 Bolton-Bury-Rochdale route. 19 August 2019. *David Barrow*

Above: 'Accidents will happen'. On 29 April 2020, 40705 SO19 MWA lost its roof in a low-bridge collision in Rochdale. When photographed here in Bury some six months later, 40705 had been completely re-built and was back on the road. *David Barrow*

Opposite above: **DBNW 40720** MX20 KXM about to leave Bury on its five-mile journey to Bolton. The origin of this cross-town service between Rochdale, Bury and Bolton can be traced back to the early 1930s, but after the Second World War the service was split, two routes Bury to Bolton and two services Bury to Rochdale. The 471 was only Bury to Rochdale in the SELNEC/GMT period, but later extended to Bolton. *David Barrow*

Opposite below: **Diamond Bus** 40722 is waiting to proceed over the level crossing at Ramsbottom railway station, one of the stations on the heritage East Lancashire Railway. The station was first opened in 1846. The heritage railway is twelve miles long between Rawtenstall in Lancashire, and Heywood in Greater Manchester. *David Barrow*

Above: **The same** bus waiting for the six-carriage steam train to pass on its way to Rawtenstall. *David Barrow*

Opposite: **Diamond Bus** North West 40732 MX20 KXS on route 8, Manchester-Pendlebury-Farnworth-Bolton, passing Victoria railway station in Manchester city centre. *David Barrow*

40735 MX20 KXV passing Ramsbottom railway station signal box, which dates from the mid-nineteenth century. The station at Ramsbottom closed for passenger services in June 1972, although the line remained active for freight until 1980. The heritage line was opened in 1987. *David Barrow*

Diamond 40738 MX20 KYE has just crossed the boundary between the cities of Salford and Manchester on its inward journey from Bolton to Manchester's Shudehill interchange. *David Barrow*

40746 MX20 KXZ is seen leaving Manchester on the twelve-mile journey to Bolton. Behind the bus is the AO Arena. The Arena is the second largest of its type in Europe, with a capacity for 21,000. It opened in July 1995. *David Barrow*

Diamond Bus North West StreetDeck 40749 MX20 KXE is seen passing the imposing structure of Victoria Station, opened in 1844. A £17 million installation of a new platform roof was undertaken between 2013 and 2015. Manchester has three main line stations in the city centre. *David Barrow*

40772 MX70 AOC is on a Sunday 472 service between Bury and Ramsbottom. The footbridge on the right came from Dinting near Glossop in Derbyshire. *David Barrow*

40792 MX70 AOU is entering Bury town centre on the 471 from Bolton. To the left of the bus is the statue of Sir Robert Peel (1788-1850). Born in Bury, he was a Conservative politician, who served twice as Prime Minister. He is also known as the father of modern policing, having established the Metropolitan Police Force in London in 1829. The statue was unveiled in 1852. The building to the right is the Parish Church, built in two stages in 1842 and 1876. *David Barrow*

40786 MX70 AOP is approaching the bus/Metrolink interchange in Bury, the midway point of service 471 Rochdale to Bolton.
David Barrow

Wrightbus StreetDeck 40804 MX70 APV is one of several DBNW route branded services in Greater Manchester. This one is on the 471 Bolton-Bury-Rochdale. 12 March 2021. *David Barrow*

Bury Market Place is the setting for Diamond Bus 40784 MX70 AON. This area in Bury has been the centre of any ceremonial activity over the past 200 years. *David Barrow*

One of the latest StreetDecks in the Diamond Bus North West Bolton fleet is 40809 MX21 ARZ, seen here at Shudehill interchange in central Manchester on the 8 service to Bolton via Kearsley and Clifton. The are now 148 new StreetDecks. *David Barrow*

The 'Innovation and Technology in Transport' [ITT Hub] conference and exhibition was held at Farnborough Airport in Hampshire on 30 June/1 July 2021. The Metroline example was one of three Wrightbus StreetDecks present at the event. WHD 2714 LK70 AZD was allowing the delegates in attendance the opportunity to sample a hydrogen powered double-deck bus. *David Barrow*

***Above*: Metroline, along** with Translink in Northern Ireland, and National Express West Midlands, have specified cameras instead of rear-view mirrors. *David Barrow*

***Left*: This is** the view the driver gets from the offside camera. *Michael Barrow*

The Kowloon Motor Bus Company Limited (KMB) was founded in Hong Kong in 1933. It operates over 600 routes in Kowloon and the New Territories with a fleet of 4,100 buses. KMB's one and only Wrightbus StreetDeck is seen on test on Hong Kong Island. *Philip Chan*

KMB StreetDeck WJ 1984 is fitted with a six-cylinder Mercedes Benz OM936 engine. The two-door bodywork is fitted with 72 seats. Is seen on route 81c You On Bus Terminus to Tsim East (Mody Road). *Choi Kwok Hong*

WS 6S1 WJ 1984 was supplied to KMB Hong Kong in the spring of 2018. It did not see much in the way of carrying fare paying passengers. It was returned to the UK some three years later. This offside view shows the optional glazed staircase and front upper deck corner pillars. *Anthony Lui*

The KMB StreetDeck returned to the UK in 2021, after less than three years in Hong Kong. It was acquired by dealer Ensign Bus in Purfleet, Essex. Since this photograph was taken in Leigh-on-Sea 'Essex' 24 June 2021, it has been converted to single-door, and re-seated to make it more suitable for private hire. *Matthew Evans*

Sun Bus Hong Kong is a subsidiary of the Kowloon Motor Bus (KMB) owner Transport International Holdings. At the beginning of 2021, Sun Bus took delivery of five Wrightbus StreetDecks for service NR331 Tsuen Wan Station to Ma Wan. The first one to be delivered is seen here at Hong Kong harbour next to a Citybus Duple-Metsec bodied Dennis Trident waiting to be loaded for its journey to an operator in New Zealand. *Terence Tong*

Sun Bus StreetDeck XD 8994 seen during its first week in service, March 2021. This one is fitted with solar panels on the roof. The air-con consumes a lot more power, so the solar panels help provide the extra battery power needed. *Philip Chan*

Seen again is XD 8994 on 24 March 2021 on the 331s to Tsuen Wan West. One unusual feature is the fitment of alloy wheels only on the rear axle, and standard steel ones on the front. *Grant Ng*

This left-hand drive version of the StreetDeck is seen here heading down the M1 motorway on its way to the Millbrook Proving Ground in Bedford, 9 July 2018. The bus was void of any internal fixtures and fittings. At the time of writing this bus was still in its current state, stored at Ballymena. *Richard Denny*

In 2019, a new 10.5 metre long low-height, left-hand drive, two-door StreetDeck was sold to Buses Vule in Santiago, Chile. It was delivered in the new Santiago Transportation red livery. It has seating for sixty-three plus thirty-nine standing, and one wheelchair place. It is equipped with Wi-Fi and USB ports, air conditioning, two tables at the rear upstairs, and a Mobile Passenger Detection System. It was initially operated on route 109 to Rinconda de Maipu and the ULA Metro Station. *Javier Ferrado*

H1001 NX21 HEV and LX71 AOS are two hydrogen powered StreetDecks at a National Express West Midlands Birmingham garage. The green StreetDeck is en route to the UN Climate Change Conference (COP26) in Glasgow, 31 October-12 November 2021. It takes about seven minutes to fill up with twenty-seven kilograms of hydrogen, at a cost of around £150, similar in cost to a tank full of diesel. *Tony Hunter*

Above: **A closer** look at the hydrogen StreetDeck FCEV H1001 BX21 DBO, the first of twenty for National Express West Midlands. These are used on one of the 'Sprint' corridors, which is a network of seven priority bus corridors. 'Sprint' aims to cut peak hour journey times by as much as 20 per cent. The first corridor links Birmingham, Walsall, Solihull to Birmingham Airport. It will also call at the NEC, which was one of the venues for the 2022 Commonwealth Games. *Michael Barrow*

Right: **This view** is of the upper-deck of NXWM H1001 BX21 DBO, which is fitted on both decks with sixty-three Italian-made Lazzerini high-back seats. *Michael Barrow*

H1001 BX21 DBO is seen here at the National Express West Midlands driving school at Walsall depot in August 2021. *NXWM*

The National Express West Midlands' twenty Hydroliner StreetDecks FCEVs finally entered revenue-earning passenger service in early December 2021 on route 51 Walsall to Birmingham city centre. The UK government envisage that by 2030 the majority of hydrogen powered vehicles will be a mix of HGVs, rail, and buses. As of 2021 only 2 per cent of England's local operator bus fleets are zero emission, i.e., battery electric or hydrogen. But unless the infrastructure is in place to support this next generation type of vehicles, then the government target of 80 per cent zero emission buses by 2030 will not be met. *David Barrow*

This Translink HEV96 mild hybrid StreetDeck is photographed outside the Wrightbus Ballymena factory. It was registered 5000 MXZ 6200 and was purchased by Translink in May 2019. *Wrightbus*

***Above*: Arriva Merseyside** took delivery of its first ever Wrightbus Streetdecks in December 2021. Twenty-four low-height versions entered service in January 2022 on routes serving the Liverpool area. 4710 DG71 VFX is photographed here about to enter Huyton bus station, new in service, on the 10B from Liverpool One bus station. They are equipped with free Wi-Fi, USB charging ports and audio-visual next stop announcements. They represent a total investment of £6.1 million. *David Barrow*

***Opposite above*: The first** operator for the fully electric Electroliner StreetDeck was Translink in Northern Ireland. 3531 YUI 2311 was delivered in November 2021, with all eighty examples delivered and in service by the summer of 2022. This first one was painted in this green version of the zero-emission livery. Along with the twenty hydrogen powered StreetDecks this amounted to a total investment in excess of £70 million. These electric and hydrogen buses marked a return of the first dual-doored double deckers to the streets of Belfast since the late 1980s. Translink intends to cease the purchase of all diesel only buses and trains by 2023. The Electroliner has been designed and built from the 'chassis up' as a battery/electric bus, with suspension and brakes common with the hydrogen and euro 6 diesel variations. The same goes for the body structure, which shares 80 per cent commonality with the diesel counterparts. It is available in 340 or 454 kWh configuration with a fully charging time of between 150 to 180 minutes, giving a range of up to 200 miles. Both the Electroliner and the Hydroliner are fitted with the Voith Electrical Drive System {VEDS}. This Voith unit is based on a powerful water-cooled permanent magnet, with a high-efficiency inverter. *Paul Savage*

***Opposite below*: This excellent** view of the bus station at the Lakeside Shopping Centre in Essex shows three of the twenty-one Wrightbus StreetDecks bought new by Ensign Bus in 2021. On the left is one of the seven low-height versions, 165 LX21 CHN, in the company of two of the fourteen standard height types, 179 LX71 AOO and 169 LX71 AOC. *Maurice Smithson*

This single-deck GB Hawk StreetDeck belongs to Translink in Northern Ireland. 2541 FXI 415 is seen here on route 80 Dungannon to Coalisland and Cookstown. In 2022, Translink had seventy-three GB Hawks in service. *Paul Savage*

First Bus have the largest number of Wrightbus StreetDecks in the UK. At the end of 2022 they had over 300 in service. Twenty-eight new ones were delivered to First at Bradford in February 2022. They are painted in this special two shades of blue livery. The darker blue is a throwback to the Prussian blue colour of Bradford City Transport before 1974. 35640 MD71 ENW is seen in the city centre on the 72 service to Leeds via Pudsey and Bramley. They entered service on 2 March 2022. *David Barrow*

First West of England had twenty-seven micro-hybrid StreetDecks delivered to Weston-super-Mare in March 2022. They were all branded as 'Badgerline', which was established as a company in its own right, owned by a group of former NBC managers and staff, in 1986. Badgerline eventually became part of First Bus in 1995. In 2018 the Badgerline branding was re-introduced by First West of England for services in the Weston-Super-Mare area. 35668 MF22 SXW is seen here in the town's bus interchange on its first day on the road, about to leave on route 7 to Worle Terminus and Haywood Village. *DSH Transport*

Above: **In** March 2022, the Mayor of London 'Sadiq Khan' paid a visit to the Wrightbus factory in Ballymena to see one of the first London Electroliners for Abellio. Thirty are on order for route 111 Heathrow Airport to Kingston upon Thames. Abellio UK is part of the Abellio Group, an owned subsidiary of Nederlandse Spoorwegen, a Dutch railway company. In London, they operate 800 buses across six depots, with a staff of 2,500. *Mayor of London/Wrightbus*

Opposite: **First West** of England StreetDeck 35668 MF22 SXW is seen new in service on route 7 heading towards Haywood Village, having started its journey at Worle Terminus via Weston-Super-Mare. *Neil Jennings*

In this final group of photographs, taken on the 7 September 2021, we take a look at the the process from the beginning to completion of the various stages in the production cycle of the StreetDeck. Wrightbus moved to this present 100-acre site in 2017. Still in Ballymena, it was previously occupied by JTI Gallaher (Japan Tobacco International). The former site is still an integral part of the production process, where spray painting of all the buses is carried out.

I have chosen this first view of the front axle/wheel box assembly, because this unit is more or less the same whether it is for a single or double deck, diesel, hydrogen, or electric powered bus. This view shows a fully fabricated and welded wheel box, ready for the next stage in the process. *David Barrow*

The next stage, which is carried out off site by a third party, is shot blasting and blue powder coating. The powder is sprayed on using an electrostatic gun, which imparts a negative charge to the powder. The wheel box is then heated and the powder melts into a uniform film. *David Barrow*

The wheel box is now ready for the fitting of the front axle, disc brakes and suspension.
David Barrow

The chassis is now complete and ready to move on to the next stage. This is a single deck diesel.
David Barrow

Opposite above: **This is** the diesel set up which is the Mercedes Benz OM934 four-cylinder euro 6 engine, and a Voith D854.6 four speed fully automatic gearbox. The Daimler Benz engine is a short four-cylinder unit at 5.1 litres, mounted in-line and driving direct to the gearbox and rear axle without any angle drives. This set up reduces fuel consumption by up to 4 per cent and if needed, the Voith gearbox can be removed with the engine in situ. *David Barrow*

Opposite below: **The early** stage of body construction. The main body sides, roof and intermediate floor are all jig assembled separately before bolting to the chassis. *David Barrow*

Above: **The body** has now been fitted with the front panel and destination box, plus upper and lower front screens. Work has also commenced on the interior i.e., floor covering, wiring, etc. *David Barrow*

The hydrogen power unit, showing the four hydrogen fuel tanks in position. The two top tanks are located behind the upper deck rear seats. *David Barrow*

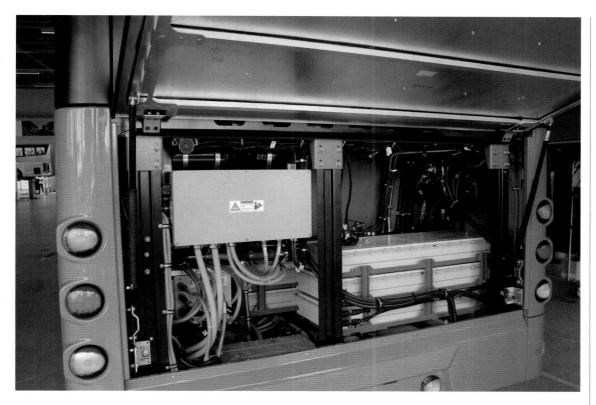

This is the electric power pack as fitted to one of the eighty Electroliner BEV StreetDecks for Northern Ireland operator Translink. The batteries are housed under the lower deck floor and the offside rear. The modular battery system is arranged in four, six or eight units, which in turn means they can be removed or added to increase the vehicle's mileage range or lower the overall gross weight. The Voith Electrical Drive System is a standard fitment. *David Barrow*

A single deck version of the StreetDeck ready for painting. *David Barrow*

This Translink Hydroliner StreetDeck is now at the finishing stage, where the interior is completed prior to a brake and road test. Note that it is fitted with cameras instead of rear-view mirrors. The government published its 'Hydrogen Strategy' white paper in the summer of 2021. It envisages hydrogen will create 9,000 new jobs, with £4bn worth of investment by 2030. *David Barrow*

A rear view of the hydrogen StreetDeck showing the roof mounted hydrogen overflow pipe on the rear roof offside corner. The steel guard is to protect against damage. The government also stated that they expect hydrogen vehicles, particular depot-based transport, including buses, to consume the bulk of hydrogen during the next ten years. *David Barrow*

Ensign Bus from Purfleet in Essex 176 LX71 AOL is about to undergo a brake test and pre-delivery inspection before embarking on a two-mile road test. Ensign have taken the option for a five-year warranty on all major units. *David Barrow*

Ensign Bus
StreetDeck 170 LX71 AOD. *David Barrow*

Opposite above: **Translink euro** 6 StreetDeck 3179 XUI 8179, also fitted with rear view cameras, was new in December 2020, and is allocated to Belfast Foyle depot. *David Barrow*

Opposite below: **Ensign Bus** 174 LX71 AOK is about to leave the Wrightbus Ballymena factory en-route to the port of Belfast, then on to Tilbury, then to be driven the six miles to Essex. *David Barrow*

Above: **A fine** view of Ensign Bus euro 6 diesel StreetDeck 179 LX71 AOO. *David Barrow*

This StreetDeck is body number AQ148. It is a test vehicle and has never been used in passenger service. *David Barrow*

This was the first StreetDeck to be built in 2014, chassis number 14141001, body number AH351. *David Barrow*